HOW TO MAKE PANCAKES FOR A DEAD BOY

Joan Kwon Glass

Harbor Editions
Small Harbor Publishing

Cover art by Jen Stein Hauptman
Cover design by Claire Eder
Book layout by Claire Eder

HOW TO MAKE PANCAKES FOR A DEAD BOY
JOAN KWON GLASS
ISBN 978-1-7359090-9-7
Harbor Editions,
an imprint of Small Harbor Publishing

CONTENTS

For my nephew Frankie, who died by suicide at age 11.
For Frank, Jody, Eden, Mason & Max, who lost their son & brother.
For Aidan, Teagan & Phoenix, who lost their cousin.
For Ethan, Mailee & Jax, who lost their beloved friend.
And for everyone who has survived the loss of a child to suicide.

Can you imagine it?
A child standing at the mouth
of the underworld
pleading
for a time-out,
trying to reason
with whatever's in charge:

No, no! I never
meant to stay dead.
I simply wanted
a sweeter life.

—*"The First Time," Rachel McKibbens*

HOW TO MAKE PANCAKES FOR A DEAD BOY

RED FLAGS

In the video his mom posted of them
singing along to the radio, my nephew looks terrified
that his performance will disappoint her.

Whenever my kids talked back or sassed me,
he shushed them and froze, watched me the way
small animals watch predators, as though
something was inevitable.

He asked his grandmother about heaven twice
in one week, specifically whether pain
disappears or if we carry it with us.

Two weeks before he died he ran away,
rode his bike to the diner, sat alone in a booth.

He waited for someone to notice he was gone.

LOCKED DOOR/OPEN DOOR

A locked door
    the day he died:

                a plan is unfolding
                he is on YouTube looking up how to shoot a pistol
                girls are conjuring ghosts
                he is writing a suicide note

An open door
    that night in my dreams:

                swung wide open onto a cottage, incandescent
                his footsteps: so much lighter now
                his laughter: 1,000 bells, unbound

                I take the doors in my house off the hinges
                so when the girls conjure ghosts

                maybe he will find me

HOW TO PRAY AFTER SUICIDE

Whoever loves his life, loses it.
John 12:25

fall to the floor in the empty house
kneel beside the bed where
he pulled the trigger and bled,
the same bed where he slept
safely for years

bow your head
in prayer to a new Holy Trinity:
Father, Gun, Holy Ghost
place your ear to the floor,
listen for whatever echo
death leaves behind

instead hear the family next door
greet each other halfheartedly
at the end of another day,
the front door latches behind them,
as though returning home
alive is ever something
other than a miracle.

APERTURE

Tidy little box, a wall
cut out. Unexpected aperture
the size of a prison window.
Nameless space where dust
hangs suspended in sunlight:
this is what remains
of the bullet's landing place.

We turn our attention
from sorrow to objects.
What do we keep,
what do we give up?

It takes two days to donate,
store, or sell everything
that belonged to him.
No one seems to mind
owning the bed that a dead boy
slept in days before.

The house sells quickly,
above asking price.
I wonder how the realtor
explained the strange hole
in the wall to potential buyers:

> *Notice this unique feature!*
> *Imagine stained glass here,*
> *maybe a picture window?*
>
> *You could fill it in, paint over it.*
> *Tear the whole wall down.*
>
> *You'd never know it had been here.*

LINE

At the wake, my nephew's schoolmates line up
    to pay their respects.
       Some of them crying, others terrified,
          holding onto their parents as though they might catch death
            by getting too close to his body, might drown
              by standing too near his casket, his casket
                the color of night sea and silver stars.
                His stilled body, a full moon.
            They stretch down the length of the funeral home's
          burnt coral carpet and wind around the French doors.
       The funeral director holds open the front door
      and the line continues onto the sidewalk, down past the Tim Horton's,
    stretches out in front of the strip mall and behind the dumpsters.
Down past the highway and into neighborhoods,
so many children it is easy to lose count.
The line is a Bible verse from Revelations
    I am forced to recite in front of the entire church.
      A lake appears behind a house on a hill,
        and they fidget, loosen their ties.
          The girl he almost kissed at his first dance
            finds herself standing on a dock.
              Behind her, his schoolmates tread water,
            their faces bob up and down, resigned,
            disappear below the surface.
       Each child holds on to another's leg pulls him down, down.
        When his teacher gets to the front of the line,
      she says *he was just too good for this world.*
    I greet each child, hug their tender bodies
    that bend so easily in my arms.
I tell them how brave they are to say goodbye.

EVENING IN THE BURNED HOUSE

> There is no house, yet here I am.
>
> *Morning in the Burned House* by Margaret Atwood

Tonight I will visit our burned
house for the last time.
I will peer into windows
and imagine flowers on the table
in a room of low light where I pretend
you have been waiting for me.

I've arrived later than I'd planned.
The horizon is already a sleepy eye,
watching and growing weary as I grieve.
I know I cannot stay,
you will not come.
After all, there is no house.

Still, I gather up bits
of invisible glass
and stuff my pockets
full of cinder, loving you,
loving you still.

I understand now
why after a fire or flood,
people return to their homes
and search for days in a trance
through the rubble
when there is nothing
left to recover.

FIRST SUNRISE

Ten hours after he died, I stood
at the copy machine with the other teachers
photocopying readings for my substitute.
I hadn't told anyone yet.

As I held the book down against the glass
to scan it, a green laser lit up the room.
My hand suddenly became an alien hand,
the air, some exotic, other-worldly vapor.

But then the math teacher snapped at me
for putting the wrong color paper in tray four,
and I realized I was still human.
I was still breathing the same ordinary air.

The Spanish teachers chatted in Spanish
as students jostled each other in the halls
or walked with their heads down.

The sun had not risen yet
on that first day without him in the world.
But it did. It has every day since.

HEDGEHOG

In early March, a night wind storm
knocked out the power in half our Connecticut town,
lines down everywhere.
The next morning one of my students
snuck his pet hedgehog into school under his coat.
Students stood giggling around his locker
until a teacher asked to see what they were hiding.
Later when I asked why he'd done it,
he said there was no heat at his house
after the storm, and though it probably
would have been okay
to leave the hedgehog at home,
he knew for sure that at school
she would be safe.

HOW TO MAKE PANCAKES FOR A DEAD BOY

First, crack the egg
into a sinkhole of grief.
Measure the ingredients,
then stir until the lumps
no longer resemble bullets.

Try not to see him
standing at your side
at age six,
front teeth missing,
pulling on your sleeve
to whisper with a grin:
Auntie, please add
extra chocolate chips.

Run the electric beaters
until you can no longer hear
his voice as a toddler
or the snap and boom
of his first and last shot.

Pour the batter
onto the griddle.
While the pancakes rise,
read his suicide note again.
Try to make sense of it
and get nowhere.

Cut the pancakes
into bite-sized pieces.
Sweeten the plate
as you scream.

WHAT I REGRET

Every summer we spent a week at the lake.
You and your cousins caught turtles and minnows
before dinner and they squatted enraptured
over the creatures you'd found.
Your cousins stroked the turtles' backs,
picked them up when they wandered too far.
When they stuck their whole hands in the bucket,
giggling as the fish flurried through their fingers,

you turned to me and said quietly:
maybe we should set them free.

On movie nights you held a bag of M&Ms
open on your lap and waited
as your cousins took forever to get settled.
They bickered about which pillow they needed,
what spot on the couch they'd claimed,
who had a bigger scoop of ice cream in their bowl,
how it wasn't fair and could they have more?

You never asked for more of anything.
Not even when your life depended on it.

I should have filled your arms with a blooming
bushel of your favorite candy,
found you a spot close to me on the couch
and asked you what movie made you the happiest.
I should have summoned a thousand turtles
just so you could let them go.
That last Christmas of your life, all I gave you
was an Amazon gift card.

I should have asked: *What do you dream of holding?*
Before it's too late, tell me what your heart wants.

HOLY PLACES

Before your birth, I searched for God
in churches and temples, lightning storms.
I wandered the stacks of old libraries,
read how-to-guides and timeless tragedies,
revering truths that were not mine.
In your short life, I knelt beside you.
We rolled playdough into lopsided snowmen,
stacked blocks up high and knocked
them over again and again.
On our sunlit floor, there were no mandalas,
no baptismal prayers or vows of silence.
Your laughter filled the room
like an ancient lyre.
Every breath was an offering
passed between us.
In your absence, I still wake,
write what I learned too late:
that there is no church but that
square of light
where I knelt beside you.

NAMES

For Charley Quinn

Today, my friends had their first child. During the pregnancy,
I teased them, suggesting that they name her after me.
July 14th is her birthdate, Bastille Day, day of revolution and new beginnings.
This is good, I say aloud, to no one in particular.
My nephew Frankie was born on the 17th of September, 2005, in Boston.
His Germanic name means *free man.* On the same day in 1630, the Puritans
settled on a name for their new home, after Boston, England.
On September 17th of 1862, at Antietam, more blood was shed
than in any American military battle since.
Frankie died on March 30, 2017.
All I know about that day is that it rained without stopping.
The bloodiest battles of our lives have been fought before, by our mothers
or by strangers we have never met, in lands we may not recognize.
The names of towns where we raise our children first belonged to others,
across an ocean, on land that for one reason or another, ceased to be home.
Boston, Massachusetts, was first Boston, Lincolnshire.
Birmingham, Michigan, the town where I first started asking too many questions,
and where my father fixed cars beside his father, was first Birmingham, England.
When my father left us, he wrote: *I was going to kill my dad, or myself.*
I remember reading it and wondering if he considered adding *or you*
before backing the Cadillac out of our driveway for the last time.
My friends tell me that they came up with a name for their daughter that will
belong only to her. Can that ever really be true? I close my eyes and whisper
her name the way I used to say my prayers in the dark.
Today in history, a child took her first breath. She opened her eyes.
There is nothing else.

NOCTURNE FOR LOST SONS

After *Girls are Coming Out of the Woods* by Tishani Doshi

Can you see them, the boys coming home
in the dark? They rise hungry from rivers
and coffins, we find them barefoot on train tracks,
hidden on ferries, wearing Halloween costumes
or high school tracksuits, bullet casings or pills
sputtering from their ears and pockets,
wounds pulsing with butterflies and soil,
lips stitched shut.
They follow porch lights like stars
as they crawl, dragging umbilical cords or rope
or teddy bears behind them, pelvic bones
inching forward on bellies of air—babies
who wouldn't latch, starved boys,
the ones who found the world unworthy, left notes
with messages like *you're better off without me.*
We wait for them outside the city, on piers, on porches,
hold their dinner plates, still warm.
If they arrive, we will unthread their lips and nurse them
or lay forkfuls of lasagna on their tongues.
We'll tell them their rooms are just as they left them.
When dawn comes, all of it will burn away.
We hold on as long as we can, hoping
the last sound we hear will be
of their sneakered-feet coming toward us,
dribbling balls or pedaling bicycles
from wherever they've been.
We hold on, desperate to hear them
say one last time: *Ma, what's for dinner?*

GRIEF IN FOUR SEASONS

Winter

Empty bird-feeder.
Mounds of snow sealed by ice.
My son's footprints like animal
tracks across the yard.
Christmas video Facebook memories.
Your voice. *Your voice.*
Traffic from the nearby overpass
blows by like an Arctic wind.

Spring

Yesterday we found your Nintendo DS.
You'd designed avatars for all of us.
I play your games in bed and dream in pixels.
Outside, flowers bloom everywhere
and though I've waited so long for them,
I am happiest in the dark
zooming in on your smiling cartoon face.

Summer

Two mallards bathe in our pool.
A mother skunk wobbles
across the yard with her babies.
Animals, suddenly unafraid,
everything bravest before the light fades.
The air is thick with gnats at dusk.
I hold my breath.

Fall

This September you would have been 15.
I finally put your harmonica in a drawer.
My children never seem to grow tired
of making s'mores. Their faces
are smeared with chocolate,
giddy and marshmallow-feral.
In the morning I empty the firepit.
Ashes cling to everything.

CHUSEOK 추석

Today my uncle and his wife will visit
my grandparents' tomb in Korea
the way they do every year.
They will leave trays stacked high
with persimmons and powdered tteok
then say a Christian prayer as the wind
stirs everything into wakefulness.
On 추석 we remember the rise of the Silla,
kingdom of gold crowns with jade
carved and dangling like grapes.
We celebrate three centuries of unity,
North and South, dead and living together.
We salute the rising moon.
I think of my nephew's grave in Troy, Michigan,
7,400 miles from my grandparents' tomb,
his headstone flush to the ground.
Every time it rains, water floats trash
down from the street nearby:
a cigarette box, crumpled Burger King cups,
plastic bags torn like the skin of ravaged prey.
If I could go back, I would claim a summit
and build him a tomb.
I would set a Silla crown upon his head.
Every year, I'd bring gifts and invite the wind
into the tomb where his skeletal jaws
hang wide open forever
trying to say one last thing.

KEEPING WATCH

One morning in June I noticed my mother standing
perfectly still on the sidewalk across the street.

She faced our house, examined something with great interest.
After several minutes, spooked by her unbroken gaze,

I asked her what she was doing and she said: *I just like to look.*
Eventually I see something that needs to be fixed.

The next day, she stood in the yard staring at the garage door
for 15 minutes, hands on her hips, unmoving.

When I asked about this strange habit,
the doctor told me it is quite common among older people.

They focus on a tiny detail or a problem that most of us
wouldn't even notice. The world becomes smaller,

limited to their immediate surroundings.
Everything in focus, magnified.

Frankie, if you were still alive, I'd shrink my world down
and keep watch. Grandma and I would set up camp

in your bedroom, bring a small light and leave it on all the time.
Even at night you'd be the only thing in view.

Eventually I would see what needs to be fixed.
As the hours pressed on, we'd build a new history

here in this room, this new world
that exists with you still in it.

QUESTIONS FOR MY MOTHER

I want to ask

      when he questioned you about heaven
      why did you choose angels
      you could have pointed
      to the tulips opening

      why didn't you call for help
      as soon as you heard the gunshot
      I mean how can a gunshot in the next room
      sound like anything other than a gunshot

      what if we'd written his obituary to say
      who he might have been
      and listed those who failed him
      instead of naming his survivors

      how can you still spend every Sunday
      reading those stories about men
      who give up their firstborn
      to prove their love for a God
      who will not intervene

Instead I ask

      why do you keep buying orange juice
      for my children when it has so much sugar
      their adult teeth have grown in already
      they still have their whole lives
      ahead of them

GOOGLING THE PATRON SAINT OF SUICIDES

It suggests close matches:
St. Rita of Cascia: saint of impossible
cases, difficult marriages and parenthood,
who as an infant was swarmed by white bees
that flew in and out of her mouth,
but survived unharmed.
In spite of her wish to join a convent,
she was forced to marry before age 12,
endure 24 years of beatings by her husband.
He and their sons died, and she was consecrated
the persistent widow, the precious pearl.

There is also St. Dymphna,
daughter of King Damon
and saint of mental health afflictions
who in 7th century Ireland escaped
her father's madness and set up a hospital
in Belgium for the sick and impoverished.
Her father found her, then killed her
when she refused to marry him.

When I was nine, our church choir director
was convicted of raping his three daughters.
When asked why, he answered:
They are mine. I can do what I want with them.
After that, on Sundays, I sat on the pew
beside my mother and sister, stealing glances
at his wife and children, in awe,
searching their faces for what might be useful to me.
I ask Google: *Why do horrible things happen?*
and Google replies: *We are often responsible.*

I ask: *How do people survive here?*

An easier question is *"What wouldn't you do to survive?"*

I ask: *Does God forgive everything?*

Yes

I ask: *Where is the saint who refuses forgiveness?*

THE YORK HOUSE

My house was built in 1780, with bricks
hauled by donkey cart, assembled over 40 years.
The summer we moved in, I failed to make edible jam
from the concord grapes a previous owner tended
with great pride. I let the vines grow over,
and beneath them, my son dug a replica,
WWI trench. At 13, he'd drag out his transistor
radio and set up a lookout point, lantern flickering
as the evenings burned away, and the years did too.
One summer, we dug up the yard for an inground pool.
Two hundred years of treasure tumbled out:
animal bones, smoking pipe, porcelain china,
some pieces etched with the surprised or broken faces
of Chinese women, their robes adorned
with blue and white flowers.
My children climbed and combed those hills,
gathering clouded shards of glass from apothecary jars
glinting in the late-day sun.
In the cellar, a crooked scale in the corner
is the only evidence of an apple orchard from the 1930s.
A man raised his family here. He pressed cider
for school children who passed by on their way home.
His oldest son handed out sacks
for McIntosh apples,
greeted each child by name as they chased one
another across the land, undiscovered,
broken things unseen, underfoot.
Their bags, not yet filled.

HARD EVIDENCE

Since your suicide, I sometimes Google you the way
I might Google a question I don't know the answer to.
At first what I find is always changing: photos your mother
posted on Facebook, your name on prevention fundraiser posters,
the announcement of your wake with your last school portrait.
Once I discovered a living person in Kentucky with your name.

As the years pass I find less and less of you.
Eventually, even your obituary disappears.
Soon all that remains: a map to your grave
and a stock image candle on the funeral home's website
with your name and the date of your death beside it.
Every year, the hard evidence fades and the memories
grow a technicolor skin, too bright and no longer as real.

A teacher at the local school dies and the school
plants a forsythia tree on the hillside.
In spring, its arms weep their sudden sunlight,
shake in the wind until they are released.
The plaque below reads: *her students were her favorite*
movie and she memorized all the lines.

MANDALA

If you were still alive,
I could try to love you
the way I am told to
love everyone:
with wonder & detachment,
hold you, then let you go.

But if I'm being honest,
I would probably
bolt the doors behind you
and crush you against my ribs,
both of us using our last breaths
to wish for an actual way
to love someone
        and stay alive.

I ASK THE PEARL DIVER TO BRING YOU BACK FROM THE DEAD

The 해녀 waddles toward the Jeju coast in her flippers
and wetsuit armor, adjusts her diving mask,
flashes me the peace sign and takes the plunge.

In the meantime, the other divers start a fire on the beach.
They squat and warm their hands as I pace and try to catch
a glimpse of you breaking the water's surface.

One of them calls me over to share her abalone.
Another tries to distract me with a baby octopus that squirms
in her hand, writhes as though about to transform.

Soon the 해녀 calls my name, waves in victory,
and there you are! Not the sad, quiet child I remember,
but muscular and lean, with darker hair: a man of 25

with a brave face and playful eyes. You swim toward me,
race the 해녀, and she almost beats you to the shore.
You look up at me like a field of canola opening in the sun.

When you pull yourself up onto the rocks, I embrace
your glossy body and weep the way I did when you were born.
The stilled volcano at Hallasan rumbles.

I whisper *How long do we have?* to no one in particular.
The other 해녀 applaud and chant your name,
mostly for our benefit. They see this all the time:

the creatures that grief pulls from deep, airless places,
offering bright, wild treasures, even a version of the dead
we are desperate to meet.

Ribbons of seaweed blossom at our feet and nearby
mollusks spin sand into pearls.
Every darkness we bear hides such small mercies.

PARIS, JUNE, 2017

What I remember most about Paris
the summer my daughter turned 11
is not the view from the Ferris Wheel
outside the Louvre or the intoxicating
aroma of Laduree macaroons
along cobblestone streets.
It is not wandering the corridors of skulls
beneath the city or cruising the River Seine.
It is not Van Gogh's Self-Portrait, his eyes
a maze of blue flames.

I remember most the pigeons
beneath the Eiffel Tower
as my daughter chased them,
filling the esplanade like dandelion seeds.
When the birds took flight, their wings opened
beneath 10,000 tons of iron
like the collective breath of every mother
giving birth in that moment
when your child is still yours,
but not for long, not for long.

TAKING MY DAUGHTER OUT FOR SMOOTHIES

Beautiful eyes, deceiving//We may die this evening//We will make it out I know//

Running through the flames//Let's go

"Righteous" by Juice Wrld

I.

On our way to get smoothies we pass the beach
where small hoards of adolescents in bathing suits
climb atop the side rails, raise their arms in surrender,
and drop one by one, into the Long Island Sound.
They emerge, grinning, slick and satisfied,
as sailboats stand tall nearby. When I first see them
my instinct is to stop the car, keep them from jumping.
Lately, no one is safe.

II.

When we get to the smoothie shop, the drive-thru line
is 12 cars long. While we wait, you play a song
called "Righteous" by Juice Wrld. When I ask *who's this*
you roll your eyes. In response, I smile with pursed lips
the same way my mother did when I came home
from my fancy New England college, too confident,
and aggravated that she did not know what I knew.
I realize suddenly what she did not say: *Oh, daughter,*
there is so much more than this that I don't know.

III.

As I listen to the song, I wince, knowing that lately
you've been in pain too and probably identify with the lyrics.
The singer's voice soothes and emboldens me,
and I try to think of something clever or moving or brilliant
to say, something that conveys to you the nightmare I imagine:

you will not find this world worthy of you one day.
The reason I take you for smoothie runs at dusk,
always choosing the busiest time of day, is that I am hoping
for long lines, for traffic, for anything to keep you
close to me a little bit longer.

IV.

You take your smoothie without looking up from your phone.
As we wait to turn at the intersection,
I could reach across the seat and touch your hand.
I could tell you that pain is temporary,
that there is a future version of you who will rescue you,
that you have to stay alive to meet her.
But what 14 year old girl believes that her mother
has answers to any of her questions?

V.

I turn on my blinker at the intersection.
Outside the car, the world around us quivers
with heat, exhausted, as though our mere existence
tests its limits. *I have been thinking a lot
about God lately,* you say suddenly.
Like when I pray, how do I even know if he's listening?
I nod my head, look left and right, wait
for a sign that it's safe to keep going.

FIRST MORNING

The first school bus heaves itself
around the corner,
an immense prehistoric bird,
pitches its hips burdened
forward then flies.
We try to read each other's eyes
as there is no language yet.
We are the first people
and today is the first morning.

Maybe this ordinary courtyard
of white stones and flowers
or this familiar brick pathway
is where we start again.
Maybe it is the front door
of every schoolhouse opening,
welcoming us in
despite how screwed up
the world can be.

A teacher takes a child's hand,
and the child goes.
Inside, maps wait to be opened.

ACKNOWLEDGMENTS

"Locked Door/Open Door" appeared in *Cross & Crow Keys*

"How to Make Pancakes For a Dead Boy" and earlier version of "Mandala" appeared in *Anti-Heroin Chic*

"How to Pray" appeared in *FEED* (Issue 1.21)

"Keeping Watch" & "Chuseok" appeared in *West Trestle Review*

"Evening in the Burned House" and "Holy Places" appeared in University of Albany's *Offcourse*

"Hedgehog" (published as "Safe") in *Porcupine Lit*

"Taking my Daughter Out for Smoothies" appeared in *Dissonance Magazine*

"Names" (published as "There is Nothing Else") appeared in *Ghost City Review*

"Googling the Patron Saint of Suicides" appeared in *Wondrous Real*

"Paris, June, 2017" and "First Morning" appeared in the anthology *Shimmer Spring*

"I Ask the Pearl Diver to Bring You Back From the Dead" appeared in *Mom Egg Review*

"Questions for my Mother" appeared in *Negative Capability*

"What I Regret" appeared in *Diode*

ABOUT THE AUTHOR

Joan Kwon Glass is the author of the forthcoming collection *Night Swim*, winner of the 2021 Diode Editions Book Contest, and the forthcoming chapbook *If Rust Can Grow on the Moon* at Milk & Cake Press in 2022. She serves as poet laureate for the city of Milford, Connecticut, and as poetry co-editor for *West Trestle Review*. Her poems have recently been published or are forthcoming in *Diode, The Rupture, Rattle, The Hellbore, Pirene's Fountain, Dialogist, South Florida Poetry Journal, Rust & Moth, Honey Literary, SWWIM*, and many others. Joan has been nominated multiple times for the Pushcart Prize and Best of the Net. She tweets @joanpglass and you may read her previously published work at www. joankwonglass.com.